Dear Readers:

Maybe as you finished your years at school and stepped into the world of work, you thought you could become financially healthy [or wealthy] with your newfound income, however, it isn't happening! Almost everybody in the world expands their life to fit their income. You are not alone.

This book is written to encourage and inspire you. You can learn and grow rich. Probably you've heard many of these ideas before but for whatever reason they just did not click. As you go through the pages let your instinct tell you what to act on. Just do it, without overthinking.

Life doesn't always happen the way you plan. As you dive into *Funny Money*, you'll laugh, you might cry and hopefully, you'll learn something valuable. Take your time and soak it up. Read a bit. Do a bit. Then read and do more. Even if you only get one great tool or idea that you use from this book, you'll be better off.

I PROMISE you riches in more than just money IF you take the actions in the book. Events will happen to you during your life. However if you read every page in this book and take all of the actions, I promise your life will change forever. Your business will grow faster. You'll find your confidence in money decisions. You'll be braver. You'll rediscover your own soul-driven purpose that becomes your fuel for wealth building. I could've used this book long ago.

So readers, enjoy *Funny Money: Laugh & Grow Rich*. Prove me right!

Contents

Introduction

Quotes, observations & action ideas

Resources

Forms

Explore your financial savvy
Take the Money Quiz

www.FreedomQuestAcademy.com/moneyquiz

Action Item

Read this poem out loud every morning for 21 days. Notice what you see in your life. If you don't like what you see, write down what you want on an index card, read three times a day. Soon you will be thinking different thoughts. Your mindset, your brain, your thinking is one of your greatest assets in your quest for all well-being - physical, financial, and emotional.

"Change your thoughts and you change your world".

– Norman Vincent Peale

Nearly four decades ago I found this little book, *As a Man Thinketh*, by James Allen, author & poet, 1864-1912. In the introduction he wrote this:

Mind is the Master power that moulds and makes,
And Man (Woman) is Mind, and evermore s/he takes
The tool of Thought, and, shaping what s/he wills,
Brings forth a thousand joys, a thousand ills: —
S/He thinks in secret, and it comes to pass:
Environment is but her/his looking-glass.

This poem and book were a slap in my face in looking at my own life. It says to me, "Wake up, SharonAnn. Do anything else but what you are doing. Change your thoughts however you can. Write them, do them. Use your tool of thought!"

Action Item

Get a time tracking app or notebook and write down how often and how long you are on FB, or Pinterest or Instagram. I challenge you to be on Facebook during the time you normally watch TV, not during the daytime, when you are working. Staying focused on your work pays big dividends. By the way, have you calculated how much an hour of time is worth?

> Do you want to make money from facebook?
> It's easy!
> Just go to your account setting, deactivate
> your account, and go to work!

It's so addictive, checking our friends and family. Just like ice cream we seem to crave it daily. Regularly I hear the words, "I don't have time to ..." This is a place where time goes. If you look at Facebook while you need to be working, then you are robbing your business, your future and/or your employer.

Action Item

Answering these questions for yourself help you get into your deepest yearnings. In the midst of your busy world it is nearly impossible to really think. That is why mini-retreats or breathers can help you uncover your own answers and keep you focused.

I, _____, am here on this earth at this time to receive _____.

I,_____, am here on this earth at this time to give _____

_____.

Recommendation: Put a monthly retreat weekend on your calendar for the rest of the year.

"Your soul-driven business will bring you more wealth than you could possibly imagine."

– SharonAnn Hamilton

You are never too old to discover your next purpose in life. Even when you might be feeling overwhelmed with career, family, exercise, and vacations, carve out a free day and take yourself on a mini-retreat to stop and dream and think and plan. You can direct your resources and your life toward fulfilling your next purpose. For a few years, I set aside the last weekend of the month, just for a mental health breather.

Action Item

One idea is to use Friday afternoons, or any regular time, to set your priorities for the coming week. I notice that when I put them in writing and on the calendar, they tend to happen. No decisions need to be made except just doing them. Just do them. Give yourself a big hug.

"The most difficult thing is the decision to act, the rest is merely tenacity."

– Amelia Earhart

It's easy, in the chaos of our lives, to lose sight of our priorities. Priorities are based on goals and goals fulfill our purpose. The most successful people in the world use some kind of system to keep their focus on their priorities.

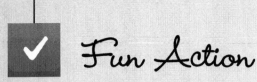

Fun Action

Many examples are available on Google images under mind mapping. My own are on a roll of brown paper or butcher paper. I like many colored pens. Although I'm not an artist, I find that getting my plans and goals out of my head onto the paper is inspirational. It helps to organize priorities and keep me on track. Try one on!

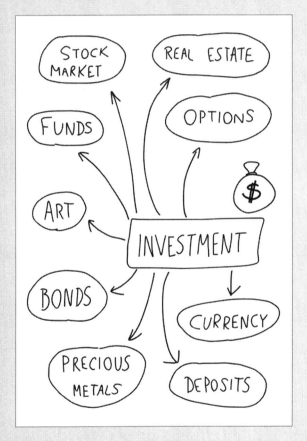

"Your world is a living expression of how you are using and have used your mind".

Earl Nightingale (1921-1989)

Ouch! Could this be true. Oh, let me go back to the drawing board. I feel a mind map coming on! A mind map is a diagram used to visually organize information. Mindmapping is both art and science. It is a way to get the chaos out of your head, onto a paper or poster so you can see your way clearly ahead. It IS possible to open a new door to a new way to create your new living expression.

Challenge

Learn more about the power of dreaming and making a plan. Start by writing your personal vision.

I, _____, believe my deepest desire, my yearning is _____

_____

_____

_____

_____

_____

> ## "Strong, deeply rooted desire is the starting point of all achievement."
>
> – *Napoleon Hill*

As a young teen growing up in a community of 200 people. I was a voracious reader. The county library was just down my street and by age 14, I'd read every book in the place. I was caught up in *The Travels of Marco Polo*, a 13th-century travelogue written down by Rustichello da Pisa, from stories told by Marco Polo. He described Polo's travels throughout Asia between 1276 and 1291, and his experiences at the court of Kublai Khan.

This was the birth of my first lifeplan. At age 14, my plan was to become fluent in French, to learn a trade I could do anywhere, to travel and to live overseas. Then, to return to the United States by age 27, to marry, to finish school, and to have a family. So I did.

Action

As you look at your financial picture, what would you need to have saved and available in order to feel like you could make a change in your career/homeplace/town/life plan? What is your own personal comfort $_____?

"Life is not a journey to the grave with
intention of arriving in a pretty and preserved body
but rather to skid in broadside, thoroughly used up,
totally wornout, and procaliming loudly
WOW-- What a Ride!"
Hunter S. Thompson

It is never too late! You meet people or read a biography about someone and the most intriguing fact is how they are able to shift their interests and passions onto a different track. Could it be possible that you are meant to transform, to change over your lifetime? When your life becomes stale or boring, maybe there is a message for you to shift it. One compelling reason to become a wiser money manager is to be able to have choices when or if it is time to change your life. When you have little debt and some savings put aside, you feel free. You are free.

Action

Action: Get the book *Think and Grow Rich* by Napolean Hill. Read or listen to it. Absorb it.

You will never be the same.

Whatever the mind of man can conceive and believe, it can achieve. Thoughts are things! And powerful things at that, when mixed with definiteness of purpose, and burning desire, can be translated into riches. Use auto-suggestion, have faith, imagination and overcome fear and time is your opposite player as in checkerboard.

– *Napoleon Hill (1883-1970)*

What a notion, to think about your thoughts. And systematically shift them, and your life, into what great possibilities you imagine.

 **Action**

Whenever I feel a change coming on I make a plan, do the plan, either celebrate or learn. Make a new plan, etc. You can do this too. The only mistakes are not making a plan and not learning. You can make a new plan on an index card, on your 'notes' app, or on a napkin at dinner. You can even make a new plan with your significant other while on a Sunday drive.

"Where is the life that late I led?"

– Shakespeare

The most sorrowful words you will hear from the old ones, "I should've, I could've, I would've." Words of regret.

Maybe it is time to stop waiting.

Action Plan

Find a quiet place in nature, pen and notebook in hand, and answer three questions.

1. Why am I in this business?

2. How does my work contribute to others?

3. What is my business vision?

> **"Most people work just hard enough not to get fired and get paid just enough money not to quit"**
>
> *– George Carlin*

Sometimes you choose to go into business because you hate having a boss or you don't like the jobs available. You buy yourself a job. Sadly, your income stays at the level you think you would've earned instead of thriving with no limits.

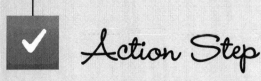

Action Step

Try the best money management technique I've ever found for clients with fluctuating income.

Take a blank page and draw a line down the left side and across the bottom

Label the left sideline $, the bottom line TIME and put twelve slashes across [one for each month]

Be honest with yourself - look at your monthly income for the past 12 months and put a dot where the month and the $ intersect

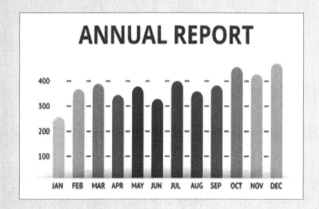

Circle the lowest income month THIS is what I recommend that you _not_ exceed in business and life expenses.

Over the next twelve months ALL excess needs to go into saving, investing and protecting.

> # I have enough money to live comfortably for the rest of my life - if i die next Tuesday.

"I have enough money to last me the rest of my life, unless I buy something."

– Jackie Mason

If your income is variable because you're in sales or you own a business, it's easy to fool yourself about your finances. Often you see the amount of income you have one month, and commit to a long-term debt such as a car or house because you want to believe it will happen every month.

Action Step

This is one of the hardest exercise I've ever done. There was a time when I could just want something, buy it and juggle the money later. But I wanted to be in control. If you want to do this, then use a book, a note on your phone, or find an app and write down EVERY dollar you spend and what it was for. Do this for three months. Add up your spending into categories: food out, drinks, clothes, gas, entertainment etc.Then look at the truth.

"It's easy to meet expenses – everywhere we go, there they are."

– Anonymous

Get honest and real to your own self.

You might think you spend $400 a month on food and drinks but when you look at the truth, you could see it is really $550. It's truth time!

Action Step

In a quiet place, consider your life as it is now. Make a list of what you don't want. [You will need this later.]

The good news is we managed to save your life
The bad news is you are going to spend the rest
of it paying for the good news!

You are the sum total of every decision you have made about money, relationships, health, family, stress, education, calling, and spiritual walk. Even scarier, every food choice you make is one for good health or bad health.

Your life is your self-expression.

Action

You are free to have some fun with this.

My purpose for now is _____

_____

My motto or personal mission this year is _____

_____

_____

(If you don't know, make something up. Pretend.)

"You can turbocharge your work
and your life this year by finding
a motto or personal mission
phrase."

– *SharonAnn Hamilton*

It is really not that hard. If your purpose is not clear, just make
something up that feels right, as a placeholder, until your
purpose is clear. If you feel stuck, then think about what you
loved doing as a child you might find some important signs that
point toward your purpose.

Challenge

Write a few sentences about this idea and how it might be true for you.

> "Many people take no care of
> their money till they come nearly
> to the end of it, and others do just
> the same with their time."
>
> – *Johann Wolfgang von Goethe*

What does it take to stop you in your tracks? Looming financial disaster or a revelation? I've had this thought for many years. If you can learn to manage your money, you can translate the same system to time and food. Likewise if you can learn to manage your food, you can translate the same system to money and time. Or learning to manage your time will help you create a similar system to manage your food and money.

Action

Write your own personal affirmation about being free.

Sample: I am free to be happy and I choose to be happy every day. I am free to choose a positive attitude. I so choose.

"Man or woman is free at the moment she or he wishes to be."

– *Voltaire*

Sure we have responsibilities to ourselves, our families, our clients and our staff. However, we're free to learn how to be effective providers. We're free to decide on our vision. We're free to make a plan of action. We're free to say no. We're free to be happy.

Action

Choose to begin simplifying. Start with one area that seems the easiest. *The Japanese Art of Tidying* by Marie Kondo is a fast, fun read and inspirational. You can do this by yourself, you don't have to. There are professional declutterers. Name three things you will do to start:

I,_____, will

1. +

2. +

3. +

"Three Rules of Work: Out of clutter find simplicity. From discord find harmony. In the middle of difficulty lies opportunity."

– Albert Einstein

One way to think about your life, your work, your business is that decluttering and clearing helps you see the real issues that need attention. As you simplify, priorities start to emerge. Then and only then can you see the real opportunities. I found my environment the easiest place to start - my desk, my car, my wallet, my desktop.

Action

Find a quiet place for a few minutes of relaxing.

Close your eyes and take a deep breath. Feel your power to change. Be grateful.

Now, write a list of what you DO want. (You'll need it later.)

"Change, Moi? When you think you can, you can."

– SharonAnn Hamilton

A monk visited New York and stopped at a hot dog vendor, placed his order and gave the vendor a $20 bill. The vendor carefully builds the hot dog and hands it to the monk with a big smiling 'Thank You". The monk protested, "What about my change?" The hot dog vendor replied seriously, "Sir, change comes from within."

If the only thing that sticks to you from this book is this then it's well worth your time. Change comes from setting your mind to getting different results than you have in the past. Change comes from envisioning future success. Change comes from writing out your business plan, your financial plan, your life plan. Change can be a choice and even a desired lifestyle. You are in control.

Action

This is a good one for a lazy afternoon outdoors. Find a tree and just sit on the ground under it.

Let your mind drift…

My life purpose has been or is being revealed to me

_____ _____

_____

I, _____, choose to align all of my resources toward fulfillment.

"You are unstoppable when you align your self-conscious, your subconscious and your super-conscious with your life purpose."

– *SharonAnn Hamilton*

Just think. If you marshal all your time, all your creative and work energy, all your money and all your thoughts toward your purpose, you'll be like a guided missile. You will ignore any obstacle. You will not be derailed by what others say. Be unstoppable!

Action

Write a few sentences about this quote.

The quickest way to double your money is to fold it over and put it back in your pocket!

The piercing humor of Will Rogers is a legacy to out-of-the-box thinking.

Isn't it time to master your money?

Action

Read *Money Magic*, by Deborah L. Price, founder of the Money Coaching Institute, teaches about money archetypes: innocent, victim, martyr, creator-artist, warrior, fool, and money magician. These patterns are rooted in our past but once we figure them out we can find ways to replace the unhealthy patterns with empowering ones.

> ## "Step out of the history that is holding you back. Step into the new story you are willing to create."
>
> *– Oprah Winfrey*

Be curious about your own patterns. The roots are in your childhood and it's simple (but not easy) to investigate. Deborah Price, author of *Money Magic*, teaches how your archetypes or patterns can be understood. Once understood and labeled, then you can effect changes.

Action

Beware all pronouncements about your money until you verify the source with your own eyes. See for yourself.

Let's use money as a tool for living, really living. A good tool that will protect you a money policy statement. This is a written document that reminds you of your goals as well as your boundaries and risk tolerances. See appendix

"For the love of money is a root of all kinds of evil. Some people, eager for money, have wandered from the faith and pierced themselves with many griefs."

– 1 Timothy 6:10

Many people misquote this, saying, "'Money is the root of all evil." They have even given away all of their money. It is not true. It is the <u>love</u> of money that is the root of all evil. You can see the results in behaviors like gambling addiction or unethical business practices in order to acquire money.

Action Step

Just like being on a runaway horse it is never too soon to get back in control. Either write down every expense you make in a notebook OR get an app that helps you record your cash outflow. Have you seen Mint.com?

Denial = That moment when you refuse to check your bank account because you don't want to see how much money you don't have

Denial is the number one reason you stay in your mess. You're afraid to look. You're afraid to tell yourself the truth. You're afraid to ask someone for help. You're ashamed and embarrassed. You're stuck.

I almost died because of a runaway horse. My good friend, Sue, and I went horseback riding on her horses. We rode up Tahquitz trail, in the San Jacinto Mountains in Southern California. It was nearly 3 miles and fast rising up switchbacks. The trail had logs embedded to direct the water off the pathway but made for dangerous walking. My horse got the bit between her head, whirled around and bolted down the trail. After we made the third switchback I knew I had to get control back or I would be killed. We headed for the next switchback with a big boulder on the left and I reach down and with all my force pulled the left rein toward it and she skidded to a stop. I dismounted quickly and we both were winded and scared to death. Denial of my real situation would have gotten me killed.

Fun Action Item

Maybe your spending plan would be more fun if you have a buddy. You can involve your significant other, an older child, a good friend or start a group where you can check in about your tracking the prior week. Does that sound too serious? What about everyone putting $5 in the pool and at the end of 4 months you pay out to a winner? Anyway making it a game will change it from boring to challenging. It would also be fun to share your observations.

Liquidity
That's when you look at your bank
balance and wet your pants

If you are a person who writes a check and hopes it will go through, then you are suffering unnecessary stress.

If you are a person who stands in the grocery line with a few dollars of groceries and prays to be 'approved', then you are suffering unnecessary stress.

If you are a person who puts $10 of gas in your car because that is the cash you have, you are suffering unnecessary stress.

Gentle Challenge

I, _____, made a mistake in

_____last week.

I noticed _____'s mistake

and take the lesson of _____

_____to heart.

> **"Learn from the mistakes of others. You can't live long enough to make them all yourself."**
>
> – *Eleanor Roosevelt*

Mistakes are funny things. First, you can't learn from mistakes you won't admit. Second, you can learn from other's mistakes if you want to. The thought of walking in someone's moccasins helps you to integrate their experience into your own awareness too.

Action

Fill in the blank:

I commit to saving $_____ per week/month. (The first $ from each paycheck goes in savings. The change in your pocket or purse goes in savings each week/month. Sell something you don't need and put $ into savings.)

"Lazy hands make for poverty, but diligent hands bring wealth."

– Proverbs 10:4

Every historical and current teacher about money show this process in action. All say, "Start saving now with whatever you can find. As time goes on, you'll have the habit and you'll increase what you save automatically." If you want to be rich, start saving regularly right now. It is the habit that is vital, not initially the amount you can save.

Action

Watch Brené Brown's Youtube on The Power of Vulnerability.

You never have to share this with anyone. Get a notebook and start writing - My Story: _____

> ## "Owning our story can be hard but not nearly as difficult as spending our lives running from it."
>
> *– Brene Brown*

I met someone who has spent his life running from his story. He squelched it for a few decades. He refused to discuss what had been done to him by his father, even in a safe place of therapy. He tried to compensate his feelings of unworthiness by buying friendships. His anger became inwardly focused until he had a heart attack. Perhaps your own story is not pretty. Maybe it is time to stop running from it and seek help.

I am not above this despite my years in the financial business. I once borrowed the equity on my house to support a business that needed cash flow and ended up losing both. It took me a long time to see my part in this catastrophe. What can I say? Am I embarrassed? Sure. I am human. I learned and it won't happen again. Did it kill me? Nope, I am still alive, still working on my dreams, still planning, and still moving forward.

Affirmation

I am happy doing my day-to-day commitments, my small acts, because they honor my personal/business vision.

> **"Put your heart, mind, and soul into even your smallest acts. This is the secret of success."**
>
> *– Swami Sivananda*

Saving on a regular basis IS a small act. When you clearly articulate your personal and business vision, the day-to-day small actions are easy. Your business will succeed. Your personal fortune will grow.

Challenge

Find a way to check your vision against your current reality every morning. Maybe your vision is written in goals. It is easy to see if they are accomplished or not. Then go to work.

> ## "Every day I get up and look through the Forbes list of the richest people in America. If I'm not there, I go to work."
>
> *– Robert Orben*

Robert Orben has a dream. Every day he can see where he is in relation to the dream. He is either there, or not there. His decision is simple. He goes to work. What could be possible for you if you woke up every morning and checked your own personal/business vision and compared it to where you are in reality?

Action

This is a big and important one. Remove ALL credit cards from your wallet except one that you pay off every month. It's better if this card is only a debit card. The end result of this action is to learn to spend only what you allocate or choose to spend, never on credit.

"Never spend your money before you have earned it."

– Thomas Jefferson

If you know you have a cancer growing inside of you would you just ignore it? Of course not, even if you're terrified, you'd take care of it right away. Guess what? With the exception of a mortgage, debt in your life is just like cancer. It's eating away at your financial well-being. Are you suffering from financial cancer?

Action

It is time to let go of shame and blame around your loss. Therapy, counseling, coaching, journaling and prayer are all great ways to find perspective and begin to move forward.

> **"Getting over a painful experience is much like crossing monkey bars. You have to let go at some point in order to move forward."**
>
> – C. S. Lewis

The most painful money experiences are loss of business, loss of job, loss of marriage and loss of capital. It's easy to torment yourself with what-ifs *but* all the suffering in your world can't change what happened.

Action

Choose to educate yourself, read at least a book a month, start talking to financial advisors until you find one you trust. Ask your friends whose advice they value. Good, relevant information is the antidote to fear. The gathering of good information is a process so be patient. You will be surprised at how much you know in six months from now.

> "Today people who hold cash
> equivalents feel comfortable.
> They shouldn't. They have opted
> for a terrible long-term asset, one
> that pays virtually nothing and is
> certain to depreciate in value."
>
> – *Warren Buffett*

People sometimes follow the media in regards to investing and because for every positive commentary there are many downer commentaries, it's all very confusing. You may opt for keeping too much cash, money market and CDs. Sadly, when you factor in taxes and loss of purchasing power [called inflation] you're really losing value on your money.

Action

Investigate and find your special place. Retreat is a great way to give yourself the luxury of quiet rest. After the rest comes contemplation and daydreams. Put a personal retreat on your calendar today. Dream. Write. Pray or Meditate. Breathe.

> **"We do not need magic to change the world, we carry all the power we need inside ourselves already: we have the power to imagine better."**
>
> – *J.K. Rowling*

Imagination is the ignition to the fire of change.

I have never imagined so freely as when I'm on retreat, especially when enjoying the beautiful and wild nature around me. You might be thinking, "I am too busy to go on a retreat." I do understand. There was a time I had a newborn, was recovering from six months in bed, had 14 and 19 year old teens in the house and my mother-in-law, ran a business with 200+ clients. I agreed to buy a business with my husband where he lived 67 miles away and I would go on the weekends. I understand busy. Fortunately the business was in the mountains in a nature reserve so I got a dose of retreat each weekend. I think the busier you are the more you need a retreat to stay centered.

Blessing

Take time every morning to name your gratitudes. Start today.

> ## "He is a wise man who does not grieve for the things which he has not, but rejoices for those which he has."
>
> *– Epictetus [AD 50-135]*

The happiest people are content with what they have.

I have a confession. I have used retail therapy. Yep! No longer, but I remember the craving. How fun it was to hunt for just the right piece of furniture to finish a room, or to improve my office, or to fill in the holes in my professional wardrobe. Oh, amazing shoes! At one time I had over a hundred pairs. Then my son was watching a VeggieTale called Mme Blueberry. The question posed was, "How much is enough?" I cannot say it was an immediate epiphany but it worked on me and eventually I stopped buying for therapy.

Then a saying on the back of a sugar pack cemented my decision and made me laugh. "If you don't get all the things you want just think about all the things you didn't get that you didn't want."

69

Action

Consider what is your plan for retirement? Finances? Activities? Contribution?

"Retired is being twice tired, I've thought first tired of working, then tired of not."

– Richard Armour

Some dream about retirement, travel, golf, bridge, visit children, and interacting with grandchildren. Then, after a time, they become bored. Could they be tired of not working or tired of not contributing of their talents, skills and abilities? I, personally don't believe in retirement but I do believe in financial independence. I've decided to be healthy and productive until I'm 108 THEN I'll consider "retirement." Nothing stops me, right?

Action

Write a few sentences to discover your own feelings about living with extended family.

> ## "I want my children to have all the things I couldn't afford. Then I want to move in with them."
>
> *– Phyllis Diller*

Haha! But this is actually a philosophy of many cultures around the world. Greek, for example, is a culture I married into. It's true, Greek parents, especially in Greece, sacrifice everything for their children in order to live with 'em after retirement. Kind of shocking for some of us. Today it's become a necessity for many Americans. Beware!

Action

Think, "What is my big, hairy, audacious goal?" Write one BHAG you have for your life.

"Far better to dare mighty things,
to win glorious triumphs, even
though checkered by failure,
than to take rank with those poor
spirits who neither enjoy much
nor suffer much, because they live
in the gray twilight that knows
not victory, nor defeat."

– James C. Collins

This goes right along with the Dream Big movement popularized in 1994.The term 'Big Hairy Audacious Goal' [BHAG] was proposed by James Collins and Jerry Porras in their 1994 book entitled *Built to Last: Successful Habits of Visionary Companies*. The idea is to create a strategic and emotionally compelling goal. You can easily apply these ideas to your own personal financial picture. When you think of your financial life as if it were a business, your management decisions will be more goal driven.

Action

My next big expense is _____. I have saved $_____ toward that goal. Or today I will spend $_____ on coffee, lunch, drinks and I have allocated $_____ in my spending plan for these items.

"Many businesses fail because the owner wasn't willing to invest and wasn't educated on the difference between spending money frivolously and investing money into the business for growth, and the risks and rewards of that cash infusion."

– Carol Roth

Your money-life is just like a business. Income less expense equals profit or loss. I've heard it called, "Misappropriated money," in referring to buying something not in your spending plan. Think before you spend.

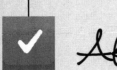

Affirmation

When I am in front of something I want right now, I will _____

_____

_____ to reset my intention to manage my money wisely and to nourish my financial well-being. [Plan 3 strategies to delay your purchase until the item can be in your spending plan.]

"The mind always rationalizes the decision it has just made!"

Anonymous

You often ignore that still small voice within in order to get what you want right now. Basically you will find a way to get what you want no matter what. This is why changing your mindset about your money is so important. The above challenge, in general, comes from childhood patterns you carry forward to your adult self. It is not easy but you can learn to change your behaviors.

Affirmation

I choose to put my worry on a paper in a box, close the box and just go to work!

"I need someone who can worry for me."

Anonymous

You can laugh, then think about this and agree, then laugh again at the absurdity. A young man went and applied and was hired right away. The CEO of the company showed him the beautifully appointed office right adjoining the CEO's office. He said, "I need someone who can worry for me. So I will tell you the things to worry about, then you worry and I will just go to work." The young man gulped and said, "I'm game." "The first worry," the CEO said, "Is how will we find the money to pay your salary!"

Action

I,_____, intend to be healthy for life and I
DO _____, _____,
_____ in order to maintain and improve
my health.

The Doctor looked my body over.
I said: is there any hope?
he said: Yes. Reincarnation

Health and money are inextricably linked. What use is money without good health? Sometimes you are in genetic good luck. Sometimes you decide to be a healthy person. And work at it. Just as you can work on becoming physically fit, you can work at becoming fiscally fit. You can make either a chore or a game. Personally, I like the game and I like winning.

Action

IF you're not where you want to be financially, then use one+ hours of your normal TV time and do something else. Learn something new. Investigate. Make a little plan. You might even become obsessed with this game. You can learn and you can win. You win when you get what you want, your desired level of financial independence for life.

> ## "You have to learn the rules of the game. And then you have to play better than anyone else."
>
> *– Albert Einstein*

A big part of the reason for the title of this book is that money IS a game. You can learn it. There are many illustrations of people who've created fortunes, lost fortunes, and created them again. They found a system, a formula that works for them. You can too. You can find something that works for you.

Make a plan

I, _____, feel curious about _____ and on _____ date I will start exploring it.

"Rejuvenate your life.
Be Curious!"

– SharonAnn Hamilton

The most youthful people I've ever met have almost a childlike interest in the world around. They are always exploring and trying something different. Different plants in their garden, different countries traveling, different spices in food, different experiences such as biking, hiking, kayaking, canoeing, classes in various subjects, learning to play a musical instrument. My Dad, for example took up classical guitar at age 72. He had classes and practiced for his own enjoyment. Another mostly retired friend of mine is interested in knitting and volunteer knits for cancer treatment patients. The world is big and you are free to follow your curiosity.

Blessing/Affirmation

Thank you that I have freedom of choice about what I put into my mind.

"Fill your mind with the good stuff. Fire the media and READ!"

– SharonAnn Hamilton

Do you remember when your world shifted on it's axis and you knew nothing would ever be the same again? When my first child was born I came home and the only thing in the news was report after report of violence done to kids. I just couldn't deal with it. So I fired the media! I find my news online or via friends and keep my home a peaceful one. I always prefer spending time talking with family and friends along with reading. The media seems to bring only fear, anger and discontent. I've no time for that.

Action

In my portfolio of $_____, I have diversified

$_____stock/equities

$_____bonds

$_____cash/money market/CD

$_____real estate

$_____guaranteed annuities

$_____other - art, precious metals

A general <u>conservative</u> rule of thumb: if you're 30 then 70% needs to be in stock/equities, in your 50s then 50% needs to be in equities, in your 70s then 30% will need to be in equities.

"If you don't risk anything, you risk even more."

– Erica Jong

Many times I've heard the words, "I want no risk investment in my portfolio." Impossible. There is investment risk, financial risk, purchasing power risk, and sixteen other risks. There is no investment with no risk. You might say, "What about a bank?" A bank offers cds but they earn less than 1% these days, taxable. Even worse at the end of a year you can't buy what you could've this year due to inflation. This is inflation/purchasing power risk.

The most secure investment is a well-diversified portfolio. The biggest security you have is the ability to earn money.

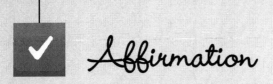

Affirmation

I, _____, am done waiting. I am starting my journey to financial independence today _____ date.

"You can't give up! If you give up, you're like everybody else."

– Chris Evert

This money management thing, this financial independence goal may seem like a long haul. It is! It is, however, a certainty that in ten years you will be a decade older, with or without assets working for your future. Your choice.

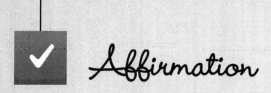

Affirmation

I, _____ choose to have a mindset of joy and hope as I work and prepare for a better future.

"I choose to make the rest of my life the best of my life."

– Louise Hay

Choices. You don't know how many years you have in front of you but they're the only years in which you can have impact, today and tomorrow. You set up your enjoyment of tomorrow by your actions today. Savor the day, and expect the best but be prepared for the worst.

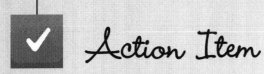

Action Item

Figure out what your numbers are:

I want to accumulate $_____ for my future monthly needs.

$_____is enough. (Use the dollars of today then find a future value calculation on the internet to see what is enough.)

"Money isn't the most important thing in life, but it's reasonably close to oxygen on the "gotta have it" scale."

– Zig Ziglar

Zig Ziglar was one of the most productive and inspiring speakers of the last 50 years. You can find him on Youtube, get books and check out his website [his son is carrying the message forward]. He speaks truth. There is no way to live in our society without money. The barter system has nearly disappeared. The do-it-yourself, off the grid, hippy types are rare. Most of us cannot do without modern conveniences like internet. The burning question for you is, "how much do you need and how much is enough?"

Action

Are you doing your great work yet? If yes, be grateful. If not, pivot. What can you do next? Open your mind to new possibilities.

"Your work is going to fill a large part of your life, and the only way to be truly satisfied is to do what you believe is great work. And the only way to do great work is to love what you do. If you haven't found it yet, keep looking. Don't settle. As with all matters of the heart, you'll know when you find it."

– *Steve Jobs*

If you are not doing your great work, keep exploring. Be brave and pivot [change direction] when an opportunity or door opens.

Action item

Bring out your credit card and bank statements for three months. You might be doing this with your new app, Mint or something similar. List your expenses, even debit card expenses on a page or spreadsheet. See if you can categorize them. Food & Drinks, clothes, toys, trips, entertainment and compare it to your spending plan. This is your wake up call. Consider your goals and acknowledge your actual spending. Which will you change?

> ## "Everyone can get a little sloppy with cash and it's smart to notice. But what's squeezing you is the big stuff you ladle onto your credit cards."
>
> *– Jane Bryant Quinn*

Truth time. If you take a look at what you put on credit cards over the last 3 months you will see your personal truth. You may not want to face it. Do it anyway.

Action item

Check your credit score often. Most monitoring services will teach you how to build your credit or improve it. The goal is to build your credit to a high point without using it much.

> ## "A bank is a place that will lend you money if you can prove that you don't need it."
>
> *– Bob Hope*

The only time we need to borrow money, unless we're in business, is for a mortgage or a car. Our credit worthiness is built, however, on our borrowing practices and repayment. If you have had a practice of paying for everything you buy with cash, then it's impossible to get a loan. It's crazy making!

Action

Describe a time you did not see the open door and what you learned.

> **"Often we look so long at the closed door that we do not see the one that has been opened for us."**
>
> *– Helen Keller*

There was a time when I was going to college and working full time at the county department of mental health. I planned to be a psychologist. After two years, I found that bureaucracy stifled me. So I quit! Chain & ball gone and a business major suddenly looked great. Onward to the MBA in Organizational Behavior. A new door opened. It took a long time to understand that I was free to quit, that I could change my plans and get on a different track.

Action items

- Plastic Surgery! Destroy the actual credit cards you have in your wallet except one, for emergencies. Define emergencies clearly and do not deviate.

- Find an interactive debt-payoff spreadsheet such as ones you find on Youtube.

- Set your mind to eliminating all debt from your life. Write out a contract with yourself/and partner. "From now on forward we vow to eliminate debt, to use credit only as per our emergency policy except for the ownership of a home. We will plan to pay off our home on or before we retire.

"The rich rule over the poor and the borrower is slave to the lender."

Proverbs 22:7

Somehow you know it is your RIGHT to get what you want when you want it. If the funds are not there, well, that is what credit cards are for. Therein lies the trap, the path to slavery. This wisdom has been known for more than 3000 years. It is time to get out of debt!

Action items

Add up your monthly expenses X 6 = _____

Create a policy in writing detailing exactly what an 'emergency' consists of, and sign it (with your partner).

Create an emergency account at your bank or credit union and save as much as you can until your goal is complete.

Then, and only then, can you move on to investing

"There are two things that you need to save for. First, you need an emergency cushion of no fewer than six months of living expenses. This needs to be cash in a liquid account where you can get at it in - yes - an emergency if you need it. In other words, money markets, not CDs. You also need to save for your future: that means retirement."

– *Jean Chatzky*

In consideration of the emergency cushion, today most people just use credit cards. This is a huge problem because the cards, in general, do not get paid off. What would you do if you knew that your credit cards were costing you 10-20 years of comfortable income at retirement? Wake up!

Action

As you think about what you want, who is going to stop you from getting there? Would you like to be a disruptor?

> ## "The question isn't who is going to let me; it's who is going to stop me."
>
> *– Ayn Rand*

There are some people with very interesting imaginations and brains. Have you read any Ayn Rand books? Writings of a revolutionary are very eye-opening. People who go against common thought are now called disruptors. If you had no debt other than your home mortgage or business capital debt, then you will be very unusual, maybe you will be a revolutionary.

Action

How many hours of 'work' can you sustain daily? _____

How long can you go when you're creatively engaged? _____

Wouldn't it be great to find a paid creative gig? Every day? _____

> **"You've got to be willing to work, and if you're willing to work, you should be able to get ahead and stay ahead."**
>
> *– Hillary Clinton*

Well, I understand willingness to work. I do, however, prefer to live in the space where work and play are the same. That inner-child and quality of wonder and curiosity is the reason I spend time in nature whenever possible.

I can put 10-12 hours into a creative work project, but be drooping after 4 hours sitting in meetings.

Action

I, _____[name] hereby commit myself to checking my spending plan on _____[day of the month] for the month ahead. If I am going to be financially in the negative I will _____ and _____ until I shift my spending plan to the positive.

(example: I, SharonAnn, hereby commit myself to checking my spending plan on the 20th of every month for the month ahead. I will either reduce expenses or create additional revenue by getting another job, selling something, or attracting another client.)

"The three most dreaded words in the English language are 'negative cash flow'."

– David Tang

The benefit of creating and following a spending plan is that you will never use these words on yourself or your business. It's a straightforward calculation: you need $X to meet your needs therefore, you need make $X. If for some reason is it not going to happen, then you need to reduce your expenses or make more money. You already know this but if you are not living within your means, it's time to take action. You have the ability and the willpower.

Action

If there is anyone in your life or anything in yourself that you think needs forgiveness, find the Hawaiian prayer of forgiveness called Ho'oponopono. You'll find several versions on Youtube. com. Just find a quiet place, bring up the person you need to forgive in your mind's eye and chant the prayer. It sometimes takes several repetitions, "I love you, I'm sorry, please forgive me, thank you." I believe you'll find incredible peace of heart.

> ## "It's one of the greatest gifts you can give yourself, to forgive. Forgive everybody."
>
> *– Maya Angelou*

There is a businessman I know who got upset over an email sent by his daughter. I saw the email and it just stated how she felt about something he did. That was three years ago and he has not spoken to her since that time. Wow! He loses out on part of his family, watching his grandkids grow up, and a host of family gatherings. In unforgiveness lies the seeds of anger, bitterness and regrets. I am sure he will be sorry in the last days of his life. It's hard to get new clients with an angry and bitter attitude. In the last three years his business has declined but he doesn't see a connection.

Circle one

I am a watcher. I am a do-er.

Consider using most of your time in groups where you can be a do-er.

"There are two kinds of people, those who do the work and those who take the credit. Try to be in the first group; there is less competition there."

– Indira Gandhi

Doing the work is actually a lot more fun that just watching. To note, have you ever watched a complete 18 rounds of golf on TV? For me, this is torture. Apologies to those who love golf.

Action

Name all of the helpers that you hire for your business/personal wants and needs:

If you don't have a financial advisor maybe it's time.

Professionals who help you find money are called financial advisors. Why not hire one?

You are very comfortable with hiring specialist to help you do what you don't know how to do. Consider attorneys, handymen, pedicurists, hairdressers, car detailers. They are ready to help. Everyone earns a living by selling what they know, even you. Even if you think you don't have money to invest, having a financial advisor work for you is a wise move.

Create a Repetition Plan

One way is to choose one activity you want to do daily to improve yourself. Write on a 3X5 index card:

I, _____, choose to _____ every day.

Read it every morning just as you wake up. Notice your new habit very soon. Then choose another activity to improve. You can use this for everything, even your financial goals.

"Any idea, plan, or purpose may be placed in the mind through repetition of thought."

– Napoleon Hill

Our brain is divided into functions: thinking brain [T] is rational and aware, the subconscious brain [S] is where our emotions and instincts reside. Studies prove you can impact your subconscious mind (that is the worker bee part of your brain) by repetition. One thing to know is that your subconscious always says, "Yes."

For example:
T: "I need a new car."
S: "Yes."
T: "But I will need to borrow money to get it."
S: "Yes."
T: "Maybe I will need to save some money up and try to get it with cash."
S: "Yes."

As you can see, the thinking brain sets the subconscious brain moving in any direction, justifying buying or saving to buy. The point is you are in control by leveraging your thinking brain. You do this by repetition of your desired action.

T: "I am saving money to buy a car within 12 months."
S: "Yes"

Repeat and repeat

Your actions will then follow.

Action

Picture yourself as totally financially independent [free]. Describe a day in your life at that time.

"Wealth is not his that has it, but his that enjoys it."

– Benjamin Franklin

In previous pages you have made a list of what you don't want, and another list of what you do want. When you get what you want, what is your next step? How do you plan to enjoy it?

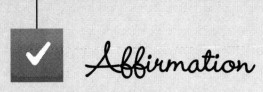

Affirmation

I am ready to face reality in my financial life starting now.

> ## "Don't tell me where your priorities are. Show me where you spend your money and I'll tell you what they are."
>
> – *James W. Frick*

The investigation of your personal/business spending will reveal your priorities. Could it be that you don't want to face this reality? If you really want to be rich, to gain wealth and to be financially free, you need to start with your truth.

Action

Do you remember your first dollar earned? How hard did you work for it?

"Keep flax from fire, and youth from gaming."

– Benjamin Franklin

There are many way to lose money but gaming, in my opinion, is the dumbest. Have you ever walked into a casino and looked at the faces of the players? No one is happy. No one even looks very interested. They're just there, addicted. I remember the first dollar I ever earned. I cleaned an old couple's house for $1 an hour. Hard work, money in my hand and I felt proud. Everytime I put a dollar into a machine, I remember my hard work and it hurts to throw away a dollar! Fortunately my kids were not interested in gambling. Now video games? That is another story.

Action

Get a notebook, or use NOTES on your phone, or make a spreadsheet and write down your ideas. Keep working on one until it's complete, accomplished or removed from your list.

> "Ideas are elusive, slippery things.
> Best to keep a pad of paper and a
> pencil at your bedside, so you can
> stab them during the night before
> they get away."
>
> *– Earl Nightingale*

In biographies of accomplished people you often see this idea, a notebook to write down ideas. One of my mentors, Deborah Price, has even developed something she calls Daily Right Action that is kept on a spreadsheet to keep us focused on activities needed to accomplish our goals. She also recommends a second list, titled 'Ideas for Future Development'. I found this to be a good balance so my fabulous new ideas are noted but not distracting me from my current project.

Action Step

Take a moment to list what's in your life right now that money cannot buy. Priceless.

"It's good to have money and the things that money can buy, but it's good, too, to check up once in awhile and make sure that you haven't lost the things that money can't buy."

– George Lorimer

In the practice of gratitude let us acknowledge all of our blessings: health, love, family, spiritual connection, ability to be creative. Acknowledge what money can't buy.

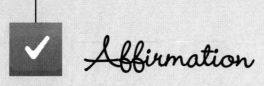

Affirmation

I'm in the process of discovering my life purpose. I'll investigate, try out new things and be open to opportunities until I find it.

> "What we really want to do
> is what we are really meant to
> do. When we do what we are
> meant to do, money comes to us,
> doors open for us, we feel useful,
> and the work we do feels like
> play to us."
>
> – *Julia Cameron*

IF our work does not feel like play perhaps it's time to find/ create different work. A key commonality of many thought leaders is this feeling of play with a purpose. If you haven't yet found yours, keep looking! It is there and you can find it.

Action

Watch as many Youtube videos of Zig Ziglar as you possibly can. Jot down the bits that speak to you the loudest. You will have another tool to use that impacts your mindset.

You were born to win, but to be a winner, you must plan to win, prepare to win, and expect to win.

– Zig Ziglar

In the 1980s I had the pleasure of hearing Zig Ziglar speak at a conference in San Diego. Such enthusiasm and joie de vivre [joy of living] came out in every word he uttered from the stage. I can hear this very phrase and his voice still ringing in my ears. He taught me to see myself as a winner. He said, "God does not make trash."

Action

Sometimes it is good to think about ourselves objectively. I found *Seven Habits of Highly Effective People*, by Stephen Covey to be helpful. He encourages readers to go through a visualization of oneself in a casket with family and friends standing around talking. What will they say about you? Now what do you want them to say about you? How will you shift so they will say what you want them to say? How will you be different now? Write out a few sentences now to answer these questions.

"Money is like love; it kills
slowly and painfully the one
who withholds it, and enlivens
the other who turns it on his
fellow man."

– *Kahlil Gibran*

Avarice is defined as extreme greed for wealth or gain. A person may acquire great wealth but in fact is not really living. Really living involves contribution to others. In the end, you take no material possession with you, but you can leave a legacy of generosity that will be remembered among the living. Big contributions AND small ones count. I feel delight when I put a quarter in someone's parking meter right before it expires knowing my small gift will help make their day better.

Affirmation

Before I launch a new business I will investigate and educate myself and work with an experienced and successful mentor.

"Plans fail for lack of counsel, but with many advisers they succeed."

– Proverbs 15:22

97% of all new businesses fail in the first year. A person may have a great idea or offer a great service but operate on assumptions that are totally wrong. Once I owned an RV park. I assumed that if I hired a PR expert and put enough print ads out into the world [this was almost 15 years ago] that campers would find us and our business would grow. Unfortunately my assumptions were wrong. Times were changing. Certainly had I spent the same amount on internet advertising my business would have flourished. How could I have known? I could have known with the help of advisors.

Are you guessing or investigating your business or career actions?

Action

Write a few sentences about your giving practice. We also give by volunteering, by helping others when we see a need, by random acts of kindness, as well as by financial donations.

"Bring the whole tithe into the storehouse, that there may be food in my house. Test me in this," says the LORD Almighty, "and see if I will not throw open the floodgates of heaven and pour out so much blessing that there will not be room enough to store it."

– Malachi 3:10

Tithing has been practiced for more than five thousand years. A tithe is generally a donation to the source of one's spiritual nourishment.

My own belief of giving a tithe reflects my understanding and gratitude that God has provided me with 100% of my revenue.

Action

Do a Benjamin Franklin Close for your next decision. Write a few sentences about the process and results.

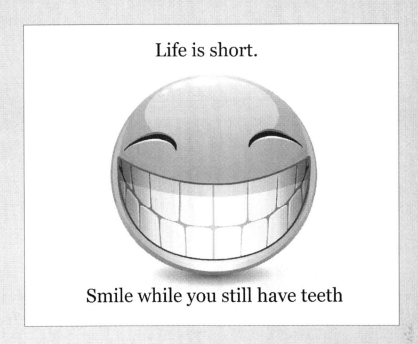

Life is short.

Smile while you still have teeth

We learned about investment risk, business risk and inflation risk but what about life risk. I've found the Benjamin Franklin close to be a great help in making decisions. Take a sheet of paper, draw a line down the middle. On the left column, write all of the negatives [cons] and on the right side, write all of the positives [pros]. The side that has the most, wins.

If you really want to laugh, understand this, "The mind always rationalizes the decision it has just made." [anon] More than likely your decision is already made. The Benjamin Franklin close will scientifically justify your decision.

Action

Go on a mini-retreat this week. Dream.

"A goal is a dream with a deadline."

– Napoleon Hill

Do you feel overwhelmed with the demands on your life? Maybe it is time to STOP and go on a mini-retreat. It might be time to THINK and DREAM and PLAN. Your dream can be a reality when you plan out the steps and a timeline to accomplish it. If not, it will remain just a thought.

Action

I, _____, have _____ years to make
my goals of _____, _____
and _____.

If I am lucky/blessed. Today I will _____ and
stop waiting.

"The trouble is, you think you have time."

– Buddha

Aye! This is exactly why freedom, financial wisdom, and planning is so important in our lives. I think that all death is premature, even when you are 89. When I was 13 years old a neighbor girl died at 15 from a botched abortion. Tragedies make you hyper-sensitive to human fragility but only for a brief time. Then you put it into a mental filing cabinet called 'history'.

Action

Do you know how much money each year you will need to be financially independent [retire]? $_____

Do you know how much capital you need then for your freedom [retirement]? $_____

> "To finance longer life spans, we must convince individuals to start investing now for the long term. But longevity should be an asset that can be levered, not a curse. They must understand that there's a cost to sitting in cash. No one talks about that cost."
>
> *– Laurence D. Fink*

The cost in lost opportunity can be devastating. The person who retires at 65 will need to finance his/her lifespan of 40-50 years ahead because medical advances increase our longevity. Keeping your money in cash is a sure-fire way of losing purchasing power over time. You will be forced to 'retire' with enough money that spending down the principle will not occur in your lifetime. You will need to diversify and make your nest egg grow even after you retire.

Challenge

What do you think you do with your 168 hours in a week?

_____ Work _____ Sleep _____ commute _____ errends

_____ exercise _____ play with your kids _____ manage your home

_____ pay bills _____ watch tv _____ cook _____ love _____ pray

Keep track: What really happened?

_____ Work _____ Sleep _____ commute _____ errends

_____ exercise _____ play with your kids _____ manage your home

_____ pay bills _____ watch tv _____ cook _____ love _____ pray

> **"Life is too short to be serious all the time. If you can't laugh, call me and I will laugh at you."**
>
> – *Anonymous*

Americans work more hours than workers in any other country. Are we happier? Richer? Contented?

Are you?

Action

Create your personal motto. Put on a 3X5 card on your refrigerator, back of bathroom door, car visor, or anywhere you will see it daily.

"MAKAPLN = make a plan"

– SharonAnn Hamilton

My car license plate, "MAKAPLN" is my personal life motto.

Keep reminders of your own motto in highly visible places. If you can't think of one you like, just make one up until the right one appears. Mottos keep you focused and keep you moving.

Action Step

Investigate your tax scenario by getting a second opinion on your taxes. Beware of someone who tells you what you want to hear. Remember Leona Helmsley, one of the richest women in the country, spent 19 months in prison for tax evasion.

"What is the difference between a taxidermist and a tax collector? The taxidermist takes only your skin."

– *Mark Twain*

The wealthiest people in the world spend a good chunk of their revenue to hire the best CPA/Tax attorneys they can find. It's also tax deductible. We can learn to do this if we want. Over my last three decades of helping people with money about 80% of my clients found out they were paying too much in taxes. We 'found' money in the tax savings to fund a great part of their financial independence plan.

Action

Fill in the blank: Think about what you purchased this month beyond food and household supplies.

I spent $_____ on _____, _____, _____, and _____ in order to have [put an X if it pertains to you] a ___certain status in my clubs, ___dress as expected for my clients, _____entertain in order to get new business, or _____ _____ [you name the reason].

Money isn't everything

It can buy a bed but not sleep
It can buy a clock but not time
It can buy a book but not knowledge
It can buy a position but not respect
It can buy medicine but not health
It can buy you blood but not life
It can buy you sex but not love

As your friend, I want to take away your pain and suffering

So send me all your money and I will suffer for you.

As you consider your spending plan, how much of this is true? Since you are using Funny Money as your part of your own journey to financial well-being, say what your truth is.

Action

Just a bit at a time doesn't hurt. Make a new spending plan and steadily increase the amount you set aside for your future. Correspondingly, your other expenses will need to decrease or you'll need additional income. You can do this. Once you set your mind on this plan, you can do this. When you transform your old patterns gradually, you can accomplish this.

"The art is not in making money, but in keeping it."

– Ancient Proverb

A good way to check yourself is look at your annual Social Security Earnings Statement. [And verify it since you already are looking at it.] Normally you have three years, three months and 15 days from the end of the year in question to correct your information. After that it's problematic. Your statement shows your annual taxable earnings since the beginning of your work history. Divide your net worth by the total earned on your statement.

How much do you have compared to what you've earned? Are you satisfied with your numbers?

Are you ready to move forward on the great adventure that is your life? Change your habits and eventually fly financially free.

Action

I know someone who treats their commute as their 'university'. They are always learning something valuable. Read or listen to the book. You also can sign up for a free Audible version and try it out.

> **"The art of living easily as to money is to pitch your scale of living one degree below your means."**
>
> *– Sir Henry Taylor*

One of the best books I've read about this very subject is George S Clason's *The Richest Man In Babylon*. He teaches financial laws through a series of stories. In it, there is a formula for gaining wealth that really works. The challenge in adopting a formula is that nothing is allowed to interfere. That means you cannot be impulsive and buy anything you want at anytime we want. Yet.

Action

Do you buy lottery tickets?

Have you looked at your odds of winning?

Action: First learn to manage money then you will be ready for a windfall.

Lottery: A tax on people who are bad at math. Ambrose Bierce

It is very odd that the people who are the poorest and can least afford it are the ones who buy lottery tickets. You can imagine winning a great prize but sadly, about 70% of lottery winners or those who receive a windfall go broke in a few years. Why? They did not learn how to manage money fast enough.

Action

Write out your investment policies. Look at them before every major financial decision.

You can find templates in the appendix, online or ask your financial advisor.

> "We are not living in a world where all roads are radii of a circle and where all, if followed long enough, will therefore draw gradually nearer and finally meet at the centre: rather in a world where every road, after a few miles, forks into two, and each of those into two again, and at each fork, you must make a decision."
>
> – CS Lewis

You are bombarded with opportunities for your money, but how do you protect yourself and your nest egg against enticement? I've found that having personal policies for investing is the way to decide which road will serve you best. Many policies are in your head but if you take some time to write them out, then you always have a quick reference, especially in the heat of the moment. Remember your last timeshare presentation? Oh, sorry it is 'vacation ownership'.

Affirmation

I choose to create relationships and connections with every person that I meet to be in a position to serve and help in any way that I can. I share generously when I can.

"If people like you, they'll listen to you, but if they trust you, they'll do business with you."

– Zig Ziglar

Let's turn this around - whom do you know, like, and trust and do business with? If you're in a sales or service business then you are a person who builds relationships. Just as you watch out for your friends you'll watch out for your strategic alliances. The more you are helpful, the faster your name is remembered for referrals.

Action

Write a list of the things you can do without spending money.

What could happen in your life if you do them now and take the money you would've spent and set most of it aside for financial independence.

"Resolve not to be poor:
whatever you have, spend less.
Poverty is a great enemy to
human happiness; it certainly
destroys liberty, and it makes
some virtues impracticable, and
others extremely difficult. "

– *Samuel Johnson*

Think on this deeply: Resolve not to be poor. Spend less that
what you have. This is easy to say but hard to do although it is
dead right.

Action

Write out your promise to yourself about funding your desired financial independence. What percentage of your revenue will you set aside without fail?

"My belly is a vital part of my 401(k)

I may have to live off this fat when I retire."

Let this not be you!

Action

Think about how your life is expressing your purpose, if it is. If not, seek until you can find it. How? Find a workshop, journal, meditate, get a coach and be open to change.

> "Blessed is he who has found his work; let him ask no other blessedness. He has a work, a life-purpose; he has found it, and will follow it! How, as a free-flowing channel, dug and torn by noble force through the sour mud swamp of one's existence, like an ever-deepening river there, it runs and flows."

> – *Thomas Carlyle*

Your purpose is that shining light that keeps you going no matter what are your circumstances. I once spent a year discovering and articulating the True Spirit of my work with my writing coach, Isabel Parlett. For me, it's about freedom, helping people find personal and financial freedom. You yearn for your life to be meaningful and wealthy in your own definition. Part of my own work is to guide people who are seeking their calling.

You *can* discover your life purpose right now. Your purpose can change over time as you learn and grow. No one else on this planet is like you and no one can fulfill your purpose except you.

Action

Get a book or audiobook about money today. Invest 10-15 minutes each day reading. Put on the audiobook during your commute or morning walk. Then get another book and do it again. Sooner or later the lessons and the language of money will become a natural part of you.

"An investment in knowledge pays the best interest."

– Benjamin Franklin

In 1981, the first career workshop I attended was in a brand new field called 'financial planning'. The leader said this exact thing: Invest in yourself first. I was hooked! Thrilled by financial planning and thrilled by the learning around it. Does that mean I know it all and never make mistakes? Not at all. Happily I've not erred with my client's wealth. I was less conservative with my own wealth and thus, learned many lessons of what not to do. I freely share them!

Action Item

You're on your way to success by tracking every expense. Fill in the blank.

I, _____ have been spending $_____ on food and drink out of the house each month. In the future I'll only spend $_____ and save the remainder. My savings will increase by $_____ per month.

"Beware of little expenses. A small leak will sink a great ship."

– Benjamin Franklin

It has been said, "You spend $10 a day eating out. That's $300 a month. When you add drinks puts that $500 a month. In 4 months you can buy a ticket to anywhere in the world. You can travel, you're just too lazy to cook."

You are the sum total of every decision you have made. You *will need to* change if you want better results.

Thankfulness

Write about the life lessons you've learned and gratitude for how they've shaped you into the unique person you are.

Now write a few sentence about your life vision and keep working on it.

> ## "The secret of change is to focus all of your energy, not on fighting the old, but on building the new."
>
> *– Socrates*

All of the thought and energy and self-punishment can't change your history. You are what and where you are. But you don't have to stay here. You can create a vision and make a plan for your desired future.

Action

Book a day or even just a morning off when you go out into nature, or elsewhere like a museum where you can simply be. No agenda except for daydreaming.

Now put it on your calendar for every month during the year ahead.

> "Thrilling ideas can come when you step out of your life for a time and let yourself imagine possibilities."
>
> *– SharonAnn Hamilton*

The act of dreaming or daydreaming and finding quiet to simply think is one of the healthiest and most profitable action you can do for a better future. This kind of dreaming refreshes and recharges you for a time ahead. You need this, at least once a month.

Action

Fill in the blank:

I am a _____ professional and I've always been drawn to _____ _____. My business or profession expresses my gift of _____ and I choose to experience an abundance of _____.

"Doing what you love is the cornerstone of having abundance in your life."

– Wayne Dyer

One of my favorite speakers on TED talks is Erwin McManus. He speaks about how and why you are created. The bottom line is that you are each unique and made to create out of your imagination. You are here on this planet at this time to give something. This gift comes from doing what you love.

Action Item

Review and cost compare all of your property and casualty insurance policies. Invest any 'found' money because you are already living without it.

I just saved a bucket on my car insurance
by switching to not paying the bill!!

You can see that this will lead to disaster very soon but it brings up a good point. Review of insurance policies. One time after a 4 year gap of ignoring my auto and homeowner policy and just letting it renew I finally went to review it. A few changes later I had saved $212 per month! My missed opportunity was four years X $212 per month = $10,178 in capital that I could have been investing. This lesson was expensive.

Action Item

Consider finding a wise advisor and get a financial plan in writing. Now. Be sure to cover cash flow, spending plan, saving/investing plan, tax planning, estate planning, retirement goals and employee benefits.

> A financial plan is a way to take all of the financial advice you come across and figure out how it applies to your specific financial situation.

"A financial plan helps you to apply all the money advice to your personal dreams."

– Anonymous

Do you believe you can make your own financial plan. In all the time up until now, have you? It is true that there is science and math behind the principles of financial planning but there is even more art involved that you realize. The art of creating a vision is the springboard of a great financial plan. You can do this yourself, but you don't have to. The art of relationship-building and trust is a key to a successful financial planning relationship. Exceptional financial planners start with understanding the client first before number crunching. If you are going to be your own financial planner, do you understand yourself?

Action

See if you can write down any messages you hear in your head about money. Then write down an opposite. Keep a notebook handy for the times these thought surface.

(example: "you are just like your father and he cannot hold onto a dime." Opposite "I am not JUST LIKE my father and I can hold onto my money."

The greatest revenge
is to achieve what others say you cannot.

You have messages running around in your head about yourself. Some messages come from your parents who repeat what they, themselves heard while growing up. These messages create behavior patterns that often sabotage your quest for financial success. They live in your subconscious. Some of these message keep you chained down.

 *Action*

Truth Time: At the last 'sale' I went to I really spent
$_____.

"Actually there was a sale today. So I saved a lot of money."

Biggest lie in the world! What was the cost? The total bill. There was NO savings.

Action Item

This week I will attack the _____ area of my budget to bring it into line with my spending plan. Once accomplished, I will choose another area. And another.

"I stopped my Victoria Secret overspending by getting fat. Now I am saving money, eating cake and wearing Walmart underwear."

THIS is pretty radical, don't you think? But it does bring up a thought of attacking specific areas of overspending. It is easy to get overwhelmed by looking at each and every expenditure and changing them all at once. My suggestion is to start with one or two areas, conquer and feel good, then move to the next.

Action

Make a policy statement for your financial well-being. What is your position for lending money? Then follow it!

> ## "If you lend someone $20, and never see that person again, it was probably worth it."
>
> *– Anonymous*

Many people have a generous nature and are easily taken advantage of. Sadly this happens in your own families, usually parents lending to their children. If you are such a person it is time to change your language from 'loaning' to 'giving'. If you are comfortable giving money to someone who asks, say "Yes". If you are not happy knowing that the 'loan' is not a loan but a 'gift', then say to the one who asks, "Put your request in writing and I will review with my financial advisor and get back to you." Do this even if you or you and your spouse are your own financial advisors.

Action

You will enjoy *The Devil's Dictionary*, as you read it bit by bit, and laugh.

"Acquaintance, n.: A person whom we know well enough to borrow from, but not well enough to lend to."

– Ambrose Bierce

Editor, journalist, satirist Ambrose Bierce [1842~1914] wrote *The Devil's Dictionary* redefining many words in funny ways. He was a cynic. For example:

Conservative[n.] A statesman who is enamoured of existing evils, as distinguished from the Liberal, who wishes to replace them with others.

Egotist[n.] - a person of low taste, more interested in himself than in me

Lawyer[n.] - one skilled in circumvention of the law

I laughed at Bierce's definitions. I laughed and learned. This book taught me much, not so much about becoming a cynic but about being aware of reality.

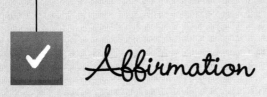

Affirmation

Slowly and surely I will accomplish my dreams.

"Pride goes before a fall."

– Aesop's Fables

Remember the story of the hare and the tortoise?

Once, a hare saw a tortoise walking slowly with a heavy shell on his back. The hare was very proud of himself and he asked the tortoise. "Shall we have a race?"

The tortoise agreed. They started the running race. The hare ran very fast. But the tortoise walked very slowly. The proud hare rested under a tree and soon slept. But the tortoise walked very fast, slowly and steadily and reached the goal. At last, the tortoise won the race.

Be the tortoise and win your own race, your own goals, your own game.

Challenge

At day's end, write down the three most important goals to accomplish tomorrow. Get yourself going early and finish them before 8am. Notice the difference in your productivity. Notice your good business results. Notice your feeling of accomplishment at day's end. Notice your revenue increasing.

"Early to bed, early to rise, keeps you healthy, wealthy and wise."

– Benjamin Franklin (1706-1790)

Poor Richard's Almanack 1732-1758 was very popular for wisdom and wit. Print runs were over 10,000 per year, an unheard of success. Well worth reading.

Since I am an early riser I would agree with this. Most early risers that I know, especially business people get all of their most import work complete by 7 or 8 am. The rest of the day they use for meetings. They may look at social media but at the end of the day or during a low energy ebb.

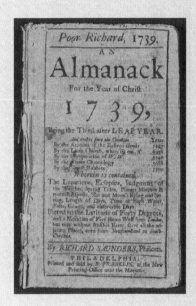

I was a young reader and I remember reading a pamphlet exactly like this. It was ragged and worn, vastly entertaining and now long gone.

Action

Honor the great gift of your imagination. Make a mental scenario, a vision as if it's truly happening right now. Seal it with a physical anchor such as touching your right hand on your left collarbone or press your thumb into your first finger. Do this often and soon just touching your anchor will bring your vision to mind. Your vision will happen faster and easier than you ever thought possible. You can do this.

> ## "Picture yourself in your mind's eye as having already achieved this goal. See yourself doing the things you'll be doing when you've reached your goal."
>
> *– Earl Nightingale*

Creating a vision has long been known to help practitioners achieve success faster. From olympic athletes to business owners, teachers and coaches all benefit from detailed vision. I call this imagination in action. One year I needed a new car. My vision was a white luxury car, leather interior, fast and save. I used the visioning technique and in four months I took the first ride in my new Jaguar XJ7. You can easily learn to create your personal vision.

Freedom is vital to your well-being. Now you have all the tools you need to achieve and maintain your freedom for life. Be patient, be persistent and savor your hard-won education.

You are free to be happy.

You are free to become anything you want.

You are free to become financially independent.

You are free to take on these lessons.

You are free to create new habits and new life.

You are free to become wealthy.

I champion you and hold the space for you to claim your freedom.

Kind Regards,

Sharon Ann

Explore your financial savvy
Take the Money Quiz

www.FreedomQuestAcademy.com/moneyquiz

Resources:

Think and Grow Rich, Napolean Hill

As a Man Thinketh, James Allen

Money Magic, Deborah L Price

You Can if You Think You Can, Zig Ziglar

Bible, New International Version

Poor Richard's Almanack, Benjamin Franklin

The Richest Man in Babylon, Richard S Clason

Ask SharonAnn:
funnymoneygrowrich@gmail.com

- Spending Plan
- Mind-mapping instructions
- Investment Policy template

Why MindMap and How

A mind map is a way to organize your thinking by getting it out of your head and onto paper. I like to use brown mailing paper because it comes in rolls. Add in a handful of brightly colored markers and a big table and you are set. You can use this to approach a single project, your entire year ahead or even your life. Many examples are found on internet images of mindmapping. There are no right or wrong ways. No limits!

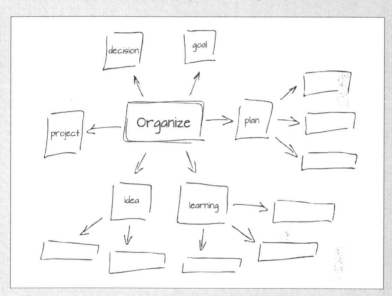

Why Create a Spending Plan and How

Why? A spending plan puts you in the driver's seat of your life's money. A spending plan helps you understand what is really going on and what you can do about creating your wealth.

How? Use a notebook, notecards or a notes app on your smartphone to record every single expense you have over a month. If you feel adventurous you can do this using any budgeting app on your smartphone. Then you categorize:

Gross Income $
Expenses $
    Paycheck deductions:
    Taxes
    Social Security/Pension
    401k/403b
    Deferred Compensation
    Charitable deductions
    Other _____
    Mortgage/Rent
    Homeowners/Renters insurance
    Property Taxes
    Homeowners Association fees

    _____

    Food
    Household supplies
    Cellphone

TV/Internet
Auto gas/maintenance
Auto insurance
Medical insurance
Out of pocket medical costs
Clothing
Education
Entertainment
Pet care
Other _____

_____

Credit Cards

Now that you know where it is all going you can decide what you want. A good place to start is to eliminate credit card debt and to create an emergency fund of 3-6 months of your living expenses.

Investment Policy Statement

Puts in writing your goals, time-lines, current assets and investments, risk tolerance, liabilities, rebalancing requirements. Most investment companies will create one with you however if you're going it alone, using a written policy statement makes decision-making much easier. See Wikipedia and Investopedia for good examples and descriptions.

Information to be included:

Name and age:
Risk Tolerance on 1-10 scale with 1 being $ under your mattress and 10 being Las Vegas $
Helps calculate your allocation strategy ie. 30% fixed, 70% equity
10+ Long term goals:
5-10 year goals:
1-5 year Short term goals:
Cash Reserves:
Retirement plan assets and allocation:
Investment assets and allocation:
Total assets in Fixed positions:
Total assets in Equity positions:
Rebalancing required: annually, semi-annually

Whenever you get a money bump, bonus, or windfall you will know where best to place the new money. Spread it out so the percentage remains the same. Imagine you have a windfall of $10,000. If the allocation strategy is 35% fixed and 65% equity, then $3,500 go into fixed accounts, $6,500 are invested into equities.

Made in the USA
San Bernardino, CA
10 March 2018